Original title:
Holly and Hearthside Memories

Author: Derek Caldwell
ISBN HARDBACK: 978-9916-94-110-2
ISBN PAPERBACK: 978-9916-94-111-9

Reminiscent Ribbons

Oh, Auntie Betty's mistletoe, what a sight!
Caught a glimpse of Cousin Lou, in a tangle tight.
With ribbons everywhere, we laughed till we cried,
In a festive mess, all our secrets confied.

Grandpa's stories spun like a yarn on the loom,
Of feasts gone awry, and a cat's great zoom.
Each tale became taller as the night wore thin,
And we’d burst out giggling at quite the din.

A Tapestry of Traditions

Each year a new venture with Grandma’s sweet treat,
Attempting to bake without missing a beat.
But flour on faces is how we compete,
In a kitchen of chaos, our joy is complete.

Uncle Joe wore that sweater, vibrant and bright,
Claiming it brought him good luck every night.
Chasing the dog while we shrieked in delight,
That poor pup, forever in festive fright!

Relics of the Hearth

In the corner, that chair with the stuffing exposed,
Where we took our first naps, or so it’s supposed.
Caught sharing a cookie, oh, what a surprise,
With crumbs on our shirts, and glints in our eyes.

Great-Grandpa’s old clock, it ticked loud and slow,
We counted the minutes till mischief would grow.
Each chime rang a warning as we planned our brigade,
To sneak ‘round the cookie jars wielding a spade!

Sugarplum Serenade

The carols rang out, off-key but with glee,
As Uncle Bob crooned, his dog on his knee.
A serenade truly, a laugh we all shared,
For music was fun, but no one's ears spared.

With candy canes stuck in the walls as our art,
Each year we remove them and call it ‘a start’.
A sugar rush painting each wall with our dreams,
As we giggled and chattered through candy-coated schemes.

Candor in the Cold

Snowflakes dance like clumsy sprites,
The dog leaps up, takes a bite.
Hot cocoa spills upon my lap,
Laughter echoes, what a trap!

Frosty noses, cheeks like bees,
A snowman laughs, just like me.
We swap tales of days gone past,
In warm laughter, time flies fast.

The Language of Light

Candles flicker with silly grins,
Shadows stretch, where fun begins.
Tinsel twirls, a dazzling mess,
Grandma's cookies? Only the best!

Sparklers sizzle, crackle and pop,
We sing off-key, never stop.
A wiggly tree with lights askew,
Who knew the holidays could be this kooky too?

Seasons in Reflections

Pinecone hats on heads of toy,
Giggling snowmen bring us joy.
A skating contest gone awry,
My backside meets the snow, oh my!

Mittens mismatched, no one cares,
We build fortresses, joyful flares.
Through frosty windows, laughter beams,
What are memories, if not dreams?

Time Woven in Flames

Fireplace crackles, stories rise,
Grandpa's ghost with twinkling eyes.
Marshmallows roast, a sticky clutch,
We laugh so hard, and it's too much!

Blankets piled up to the moon,
A cat steals space, and we all swoon.
The time ticks by, a joyful race,
In this warm hug, we find our place.

Gathered Around the Flame

We roast marshmallows, a gooey delight,
And argue who's winning the ghost story fight.
A cat steals a donut, with stealth so sly,
As laughter erupts, oh my, how we cry!

The dog wears a sweater, two sizes too small,
He’s prancing like royalty, taking it all.
We take turns in telling our most silly tales,
While the clock on the wall glares and fails.

The Night’s Gentle Embrace

With blankets piled high, we settle in tight,
But popcorn keeps flying; oh, what a sight!
A soft snore behind us, our friend takes a nap,
While we plot to prank him, oh, what a trap!

The lights start to flicker, a technical glitch,
And someone says, 'Quick! Is it a witch?'
Amidst all the chaos, a chuckle we share,
As shadows get silly, and scares turn to flair.

Twinkling Stars and Silent Wishes

Outside, stars twinkle, the world seems so wide,
But in here, our dreams are all set aside.
We’re not making wishes, just snacks by the score,
In pajama attire, it's a comfort galore!

A game of charades erupts with a bang,
The silent expressions, oh, how they hang!
We mimic a lion, then dance like a fool,
While the dog joins in, breaking every rule.

Candles in the Quiet

The candles are lit, casting shadows so tall,
But who turned the lights off? Oh dear, not at all!
The cake is a mess, but we snack with glee,
As frosting flies by, like a jubilant spree!

With jokes and with giggles, the night carries on,
And suddenly, someone bursts out in song.
Though voices are off key and laughter does rise,
In this cozy chaos, our hearts feel so wise.

Fireside Musings

The flames dance wild, a cheeky little sight,
They pop like popcorn, bursting with delight.
S'mores on the table, chocolate stacked high,
While marshmallows melt, oh my, oh my!

Grandpa's old stories make the kids laugh loud,
Like a jester performing before a big crowd.
The cat steals a treat, oh what a surprise,
As laughter erupts, and we roll our eyes!

The couch is a fort, pillows stacked just so,
A castle of comfort where giggles will flow.
With snacks in our hands, we forget all our cares,
As we plot our next heist for the cookies upstairs!

Eventually we crash, all snuggly and tight,
With dreams of grand feasts, a most comical sight.
Yet in the cool dawn, as the embers fade out,
We'll wake for more mischief, of that there's no doubt!

Cozy Corners

In a corner nook with blankets piled high,
We watch the shadows dance and flutter by.
Tea in our hands, we sip and conspire,
To cook up a plot that’s sure to backfire!

The dog steals my snack, what a sneaky old chap,
While Auntie insists on a game of the map.
Navigating the world one biscuit at a time,
With laughter so loud, it's quite the sweet crime!

A tickle fight breaks, it's chaos galore,
As we tumble and giggle right down to the floor.
The popcorn shoots out, a tasty house flurry,
And our kitty just sits, watching in a hurry!

As night wraps around us in a snuggly embrace,
We dream of tomorrow, a silly chase.
For in these warm corners, with laughter in store,
We find the sweet moments we always adore!

Frosted Wishes

In the kitchen, cookies bound,
Sprinkles flying all around.
Dad lost track of time, you see,
Made a mountain of burnt decree.

With snowflakes swirling in the air,
Mom found pie, a sweet affair.
But Uncle Bob brings in the cheese,
Now it smells like old, stinky peas.

The dog snatched one, a daring feat,
Grandma's slippers now on his feet.
Laughter echoes, stories spun,
As we share the joy of fun.

In this chaos, life unfolds,
With sweet moments, never sold.
Hoping for snow, oh what a wish,
Next year, let’s make a salmon dish!

Gathering Around the Glow

We gather ‘round that ancient chair,
Sipping cocoa, tales to share.
Someone tripped over the cat,
Now we jest, 'He’s found a mat!'

The lights blink out — a ghostly scene,
Dad yells, 'Hey, I’m not that keen!'
A flashlight shines, the laughter grows,
As shadows dance and everyone doze.

Grandma's stories get outrageous,
Once she danced with a cactus.
In the corner, the tree leans low,
As sibling bickering steals the show.

This glow brings warmth and silly cheer,
A family gathering, oh so dear.
Through laughter, every glitch we mend,
In this light, chaos is our friend.

Heartbeats in the Candlelight

Candles flicker, shadows play,
Mom’s hairdo looks like a bouquet.
We wonder how the turkey flopped,
While Uncle Jim just never stopped.

Grandpa crochets a yarn with flair,
Ends up tangled in his own hair.
We roll in laughter, tears we weep,
No one understands – what’s that beep?

The table squeaks, it’s quite a sight,
With jiggly jello and pies just right.
A toast to burns that almost *were*,
While Grandpa snores, his words a blur.

In this light of joy and jest,
Each heartbeat marks a crazy quest.
With each chuckle, bonds grow tight,
Our funny dreams take endless flight.

A Canvas of Cozy

On this day, we paint with cheer,
Each brush and giggle loud and clear.
Grandma's knitting wildly sways,
While kids create their own bouquet.

The couch is lost beneath the snacks,
Someone's pants got stuck in cracks.
Laughter bubbles, everyone talks,
As we dodge the festive socks.

Mom's dance moves, awkwardly grand,
Rival Dad's oversalted brand.
Oh, how we squeal with sheer delight,
As we invent new food-fight height.

Amidst the chaos, warmth we find,
In every moment, sweetly intertwined.
Let's canvas life with joy and glee,
A splendid mess, just let it be!

Whispers of Winter's Embrace

Snowflakes dance like quirky sprites,
Wrap your scarf, hold on tight.
Hot cocoa spills, a messy treat,
Laughter echoes, life is sweet.

Sledding down the neighbor's hill,
Geese are honking, what a thrill!
Fuzzy socks in mismatched pairs,
Socks and slippers, winter wear cares.

Old mittens lost, now on a quest,
Chasing pets, a woolly jest.
Cardboard sleds are now our pride,
With squeals of joy, we slip and slide.

A snowman with a carrot nose,
Winks at us as mischief flows.
Together we create our tales,
In winter's grip, our laughter sails.

Flickering Flames of Yesteryear

Flames flicker, shadows play,
Tales of fire light the way.
A dancing ember's sassy wink,
Milk from cookies – what a link.

Grandpa's stories fill the night,
About the cat that caused a fright.
Younger me hid, so very small,
Imagining monsters in the hall.

Popcorn kernels start to pop,
Falling tantrums, we can't stop.
With every laugh, a memory blooms,
The smell of apples, cinnamon looms.

Board games stacked in disarray,
Who'll outsmart who? Let's play!
Time slips by, yet here we stay,
Sharing warmth, come what may.

Echoes Through the Evergreen

Forest whispers on the breeze,
Spruce and fir, their stories tease.
A squirrel in a winter coat,
Skips around, like he's a goat.

With snowballs soft, we launch the fight,
Hide-and-seek until it's night.
A wild chase, a playful shove,
Linked together, laughter above.

Pinecone trophies held up high,
Fumble fingers, oh my, oh my!
Treasure hunts beneath the trees,
Nature's gifts, we find with ease.

Twilight dances, shadows weave,
Under stars, we won't believe.
Whispers spread as laughter blends,
In evergreen hugs, joy never ends.

Warmth in the Chill of Night

The windows frost with stories bright,
A world aglow in the quiet night.
Cardboard castles rise with cheer,
Radiate warmth, that's what we hear.

Blanket forts of fabric gold,
Every secret whispered told.
Shadow puppets take their stand,
Giggles shared, hand-in-hand.

Toast it up, the bread's gone wild,
A marshmallow mountain – the fire smiled.
Burnt edges, a yet-to-be feast,
S'mores galore, to say the least.

Counting stars through blankets wide,
Bedtime stories, tales that glide.
In every giggle, every fright,
We find magic in the night.

Serenity of Winter Nights

In the stillness, snowflakes fall,
A cat in a hat thinks she's so tall.
The dog in pajamas, dreaming away,
Thinks he's a reindeer, ready to play.

Hot cocoa spills as the kids all cheer,
While dad steals sips, oh so sincere.
Mom's in the kitchen, a floury mess,
Swearing next year, she'll plan for less!

Flurries of Togetherness

The snowman's nose is a carrot once lost,
A fight for the best mittens, what a cost.
The snowball fight starts, with cheers and a scream,
As Mom throws one right, it's the ultimate dream!

Laughter erupts as they tumble and roll,
Dad's in the game, just don't lose control.
A snow fort is built, with a secret trap,
To capture the dad who's snoring; oh snap!

A Flicker in Time

The lights on the tree blink a rhythm so sly,
Grandma's old stories make time slip by.
The cat feels neglected, just wants a warm lap,
While Uncle Bob naps, fell fast in a flap.

A fire crackles, a dance with the smoke,
As Aunt Lisa tells jokes that nobody pokes.
The cookie jar’s empty, we all shake our heads,
Grandpa just grins, with crumbs on his threads.

Nostalgic Glimmers

In the attic, we found that old, dusty box,
With photos and giggles, and worn-out old socks.
The costumes we wore for that one special night,
Brought laughter and memories, pure delight.

We danced like the stars in a wild, lovely trance,
Trying the moves we all learned from the dance.
Hot chocolate spilled right down cousin Ray’s back,
We all burst in laughter, what a goofy knack!

Rustic Rhythms

In the kitchen, pies go flying,
Grandma's laughter, nearly crying.
The dog snags a fruitcake treat,
Then trips on his own two feet.

Uncle Joe's socks, mismatched and bright,
Confound the family, what a sight!
He claims it's fashion, we all agree,
It’s just his way to be carefree.

Twinkling lights on every beam,
Cousins plotting up a scheme.
The cat in a box, hidden and sly,
Jumps out and makes the whole world cry.

Snowmen standing, hats askew,
With carrots stolen, just for you.
We giggle at the shapes we find,
In this crazy scene, we’re all intertwined.

Snowflakes on the Windowsill

Outside the snowflakes twist and play,
While hot cocoa spills, oh what a day!
Socks are wet from the snowball fight,
And all the pets join in with delight.

Granny's knitting, tangled yarn,
The cat thinks it’s a brand new charm.
Purls and knits become a maze,
We laugh till we cry in a winter blaze.

Frosty patterns on window glass,
We scribble love notes, oh how they pass!
Our silly glances, cheeks all aglow,
The cold can't touch the warmth from below.

Chasing snowflakes as they swirl,
With a dancing friend, we give a twirl.
The days may fade but laughter lingers,
And warmth surrounds us, home with fingers.

Stories Wrapped in Flannel

Cozy blankets piled high in a chair,
With stories old, we gather there.
The tales of ghosts with a pinch of fun,
They scare us all until we run.

Dad's old flannel, too big to wear,
A pillow fort, we just don't care.
Underneath the lights we play,
Imagining worlds that drift away.

Hot cider bubbles on the stove,
A recipe shared with the family love.
Each sip a giggle, each laugh a cheer,
Time spent drifting brings us near.

By the fire, tales unfold,
Of mishaps funny and adventures bold.
Wrapped in warmth with smiles that span,
Together forever, a jolly clan.

Memories Beneath the Garland

Garland drapes on the crooked tree,
While ornaments dance like they're wild and free.
Uncle Phil claims he still believes,
In gifts from legends that no one leaves.

The dog caught a candy cane, oh no!
Now sugar's stuck in his nutty toe.
We giggle as he hops and spins,
His antics surely are wins for wins.

Whispers of jokes float through the air,
As stories weave 'round a winter chair.
A knitted cap falls onto the floor,
And grandma chuckles, asking for more.

Clinking glasses, toasts go 'round,
With jests and laughter, a joyous sound.
In all the chaos, love prevails,
In silly moments, together, we sail.

Joy Within the Flames

When the fire crackles, we all gather near,
With marshmallows roasting, there's nothing to fear.
Stories of clumsiness make laughter ignite,
While the cat knocks the snacks down, an unplanned delight.

Grandpa’s tall tales of his youthful bravado,
Turn into giggles over help from a shadow.
We cover our mouths, not to let it all slip,
As he swears it was skill, not a comical trip.

Buttons and Boughs

Strung up like ornaments, we hang in delight,
Grandma’s old buttons shine snugly, just right.
A squirrel steals one and dashes up a tree,
Leaving us chuckling, ‘That’s quite an esprit!’

Beneath the twinkling lights, the chaos unfolds,
Uncle Ted tries to dance but slips, oh so bold.
We roll with laughter, as he lands with a thud,
In a pile of old blankets, pillows, and mud.

Rustling Memories

Rustle of wrapping, paper flying around,
A dog with a bow is the sight that we found.
Presents are bumbled, and ribbons entwined,
Each moment's a giggle, like cheese with a rind.

Aunt Jane, in her reindeer onesie so bright,
Tripped over the tree skirts, a comical sight.
Laughter erupts like a well-shaken soda,
As she pulls off her cape, "I swear I'll take Nova!"

Shared Spirits

With mugs full of cocoa, the mischief begins,
The dog jumps for joy as the chaos spins.
Eggnog spills over from all of the yells,
Every time cousin clumsily dispels.

Silly sweater contests get louder each year,
A barking brigade of fun, never severe.
We claim victory, though the results are all fluff,
In the warmth of our circle, we always have enough.

Threads of Tradition and Joy

Grandma's recipe, a bit offbeat,
Last year's fruitcake, still can't be beat.
A pinch of laughter, a sprinkling cheer,
Watch Uncle Joe dance, oh dear, oh dear!

A sock full of gifts, all wrinkled and worn,
A jug of old cider, slightly forlorn.
The dog steals the turkey, just can't resist,
We chase him in circles, like it’s on a list.

The tree leans a bit, an unruly sight,
With ornaments placed in a haphazard fight.
Grandpa will snore when the carols begin,
But just wait for dessert, that's where we win!

As candles drip wax, the laughter will flow,
Sharing wild stories that will surely grow.
Another year’s passed, with quirks and delight,
Let’s pop some more popcorn, and stay up all night!

Warmth in the Heart's Corner

The fireplace crackles, with sticks piled high,
A cat in the corner, pretending to fly.
Cousin Lou's new sweater, too tight on his frame,
His wish to fit in, a yearly old game.

The snowflakes are swirling, but there’s no real chill,
They melt with the chaos, the laughter, the thrill.
Mom’s out of eggnog, it’s quite a fiasco,
The kids are now plotting to catch a big faux-pas go.

A game of charades turns clumsy and wild,
Uncle Bob’s impression, of a dolphin-child.
Once all the wrapping paper flies in the air,
We’re stuffed, we’re all giggling, no worry, no care.

With each silly joke shared around the old chair,
We hold on to moments, inscribed here and there.
As evening tiptoes in, with cheer, smiles so bright,
Let’s toast to the nonsense, and how it feels right!

Captured in the Glow of December

The lights on the tree twinkle with glee,
But two strands are missing, oh woe is me!
Last year's toys are still here in a heap,
Surprise birthday parties we always keep.

Sipping hot cocoa, marshmallows afloat,
Trying to balance, on a wobbly boat.
A mitten goes missing, a shoe in the stew,
We toss it all out, then we laugh 'til we're blue.

The mistletoe hangs, an awkward plight,
We dodge and we weave in the soft, amber light.
Dad's telling the tales that don't seem to end,
When the clock strikes midnight, we just might offend.

But with awkwardness here, it's a family rite,
We cherish these moments that fill us with light.
In this playful chaos, love always will soar,
As we gather each year, we crave just a bit more!

Memories Wrapped in Wool

In sweaters so itchy, we dance in delight,
The dog in a bowtie, a hilarious sight!
Uncle Ted's festive hat, just slightly askew,
The kids roll their eyes, but they laugh too.

An old photo album, pages worn and frail,
Each snapshot a treasure, a moment to hail.
A snowman’s abduction, the kids on a quest,
To rescue his scarf, it’s quite a jest!

Thanksgiving leftovers now turned into stew,
Dad's experimenting, unsure what to do.
With laughter around, and stories to share,
We weave through the evening, with time to spare.

As dreams start to crown, and the night hums low,
We bundle in blankets, cozy just so.
With each funny moment, a new tale begins,
Wrapped in warm memories, that always wins!

The Quilt of Togetherness

A patchwork of laughter, stitched with care,
Grandma's secret recipe, we all must share.
A fight over the last piece of chocolate delight,
Ends with warm giggles late into the night.

Every corner crinkles with a funny old tale,
Of Uncle Joe's dancing, which never could fail.
The fabric holds stories, old and new,
Each thread's a reminder of family woohoo!

Stains of pizza sauce and unguarded juice,
Add character to fibers that never let loose.
We wrap up in warmth, both silly and bright,
In this quilt of our love, everything feels right.

With occasional snoring, the night drifts away,
As dreams of our antics begin to play.
Together we chuckle, snug on the floor,
In our quilt we'll stay, forevermore.

Candles in the Quiet

Flickering flames casting shadows so grand,
Mom's forgetful fingers with wax in her hand.
A moment of silence, then chaos erupts,
As Dad sings a song that nobody trusts.

Wick snapped like a twig, oh what a sight!
Is it a candle or a safety flight?
The dog gives a howl, sensing the fright,
As we breathe in the aroma of burnt-out delight.

Sipping on cocoa, the marshmallows float,
Not one but three on Aunt Sue's old coat.
Stirring the mix with deliberate flair,
Each sip filled with laughter, floating in air.

An unguarded wink, a tip over the table,
The flicker of light says we are quite able.
In this gentle dance of shadows and fun,
We cherish these moments, all together as one.

Glimmers of a Loved Ones' Embrace

Twinkling lights twirl like we once did,
Grandpa trips over the cat, what a big skid!
With giggles erupting, the tree loses a bow,
And Aunt Linda’s mad but can’t help but wow.

In this colorful mess, full of shine,
Cousins play tag, sipping soda and brine.
Our family of goofballs fits like a glove,
Each moment glimmers, wrapped tight with love.

Reflections dance awkwardly on the floor,
As Uncle Ed tries to showcase a roar.
Lost in the echoes of cheerful charades,
These cherished delights linger, never to fade.

Mom’s sharing her stories, precise as a map,
While Dad’s off somewhere, taking a nap.
In these golden glimmers, we’re never apart,
Each chuckle and wink is a beat of the heart.

Frost-kissed Reflections

Outside the snow falls like confetti from Heaven,
While we argue on how much dessert is eleven.
The window panes glisten, frosty and bright,
A war with snowballs is soon to ignite.

Grandpa’s snug cap has taken a flight,
Across the yard, into the dim northern light.
Caught in the fun, and completely unfazed,
He soup-ski's on ice with a flair that's crazed.

The sled is a rocket, with laughter it flies,
Mom’s face goes pink like the frosted sunrise.
We pile on together, not one bit of fear,
When streaking downhill, the thrill’s crystal clear.

Crumbs of gingerbread linger on lips,
While memories form tighter in frosty tight grips.
Through snorts and wild chuckles, we cheer and we cheer,
In these frost-kissed reflections, we hold them dear.

The Pine-scented Chronicle

In a forest where the trees stand tall,
A squirrel donned a scarf, feeling quite small.
He tried to throw snowballs, what a sight!
But every toss ended with a face full of white.

The owls hooted laughter, they couldn't believe,
As he slipped on his tail, trying to weave.
A jumble of giggles echoed through the woods,
Nature's own sitcom, bringing all kinds of moods.

Meanwhile, in the cabin, hot cocoa flew,
Marshmallows battling in the mug like they do.
Grandpa slipped, but slid right on his feet,
Singing jolly tunes while dodging the heat.

Oh, the memories we make, in the cold and the frost,
With antics that shimmer, no moment is lost.
So raise a cheer to the fun that we find,
In moments of laughter, forever entwined.

Sledding Down Memory Lane

Sleds lined up like ducks at the hilltop,
With kids bundled tight, ready to plop.
Billy took charge, yelled, "Onward we go!"
But tripped on a stick, down the slope he did flow.

Shrieks of delight mixed with giggles galore,
As they flew past the dog, who couldn’t ignore.
He chased after them, barking with glee,
While Grandma just watched, sipping her tea.

Each ride down the slope, a wild parka dance,
With faces aglow, as they all took a chance.
The first big wipeout brought tears, not of sorrow,
But howling laughter of planned chaos tomorrow.

So come join the sledding, feel life’s joyous spin,
With memories crafted through laughter and grin.
When snowflakes are falling and spirits are bright,
There’s magic in moments, and all feels just right.

Ashes and Embers

Gathered 'round the fire, we toast with delight,
While marshmallows dance, to the crackles of night.
Uncle Joe's telling tales, his hat slightly askew,
About the time he swam in the lake, but it was blue.

The flames flicker gently, casting shadows so wide,
Cousins canoodle, and they never hide.
In truths like these, legends are spun,
Like Aunt May's fruitcake, a battle not won.

As the embers glimmer, sparks raising to flight,
We remember the time when the dog took a bite.
Of Uncle Joe's sandwich, oh what a thrill,
He shrieked and he danced, but got stuck on the grill.

So here's to the flames and the stories they share,
With laughter and love, filling up the air.
With ashes now settled, our hearts linked by cheer,
In the warmth of the fire, there's nothing to fear.

The Warmth of Togetherness

In a cozy old house, blankets piled high,
We share funny stories that make us all cry.
A game of charades, where Dad can’t keep straight,
Pretending he’s flying, then tripping on fate.

The rally of laughter no one can contain,
As Grandma’s sweet dog weaves through the chain.
Like a furry tornado, chaos unguessed,
“Is it a bird? Is it a plane?” everyone guessed.

With cookies left baking and tales on the go,
A dance break erupts, scattering dough.
While the oven is beeping, and lights shine bright,
Every face is aglow, hearts cozy and light.

So let’s savor these moments, let laughter resound,
For in gatherings like this, love truly abounds.
Close friends and dear family, forever our team,
In the laughter we weave, we find our sweet dream.

Pictures of Winter's Embrace

Frosty noses and snowball fights,
Sleds zooming down frosty heights.
That one time, I fell in the snow,
My friends laughed, much to my woe.

Cocoa mugs stacked high and tall,
When we spilt some, it caused a brawl.
Marshmallows floated like boats in cream,
We all giggled, a sugary dream.

Snowmen that wobbled, then fell with a thump,
We dressed them in scarves, oh, what a lump!
With carrots for noses and rocks for their eyes,
We posed for photos, all laughing in surprise.

The chill in the air brought friends close together,
In woolly socks, we braved the cold weather.
Around the fire with stories we shared,
In the warmth of our laughter, no one felt scared.

Joy in the Twilight

Twilight dances, all colors ablaze,
With giggles and snacks, we bask in the haze.
A game of charades turned into a mess,
As Aunt Edna claimed, she's the best in the dress.

Battling shadows with fierce little lights,
We chased off the gloom with our spirited fights.
The dog joined in, thinking it's all just a game,
We laughed as he tripped, oh, what a shame!

With popcorn and pillows, we built quite the fort,
Stories of pirates gave mighty support.
Every creak in the house became a monster's sound,
But in silly scares, our joy is found.

The clock struck too soon, it wasn't quite fair,
But memories lingered, perfumed in the air.
We waved our goodbyes, hearts full of delight,
Until next time, we'll cherish this night.

Petals of Past Years

In gardens of laughter, we planted our dreams,
Silly little secrets, whispered like streams.
Picking daisies with crowns made of glee,
In moments so simple, forever we'll be.

We flew kites like birds on a string up high,
While dodging the antics of the curious sky.
Our kite dropped down, tangled in a tree,
We blamed the wind, it laughed silently.

From summers of sunshine to winter's gray chills,
We crafted our stories, shared all the thrills.
Using crayons to color our childhood so bright,
Who knew those scribbles would bring such delight?

With petals we scattered, and wishes we made,
Each laugh is a blossom that never will fade.
In the garden of time, we wander with ease,
Collecting our treasures like wisps in the breeze.

The Rhythm of Fireside Chats

By the fire, we gather, tales swirling like smoke,
With Grandpa's wild stories, laughter we stoke.
He claims he once wooed a bear in a dance,
But it's hard not to giggle; can bears really prance?

Old Aunt Betty joins with her off-key song,
We cheer her on, though it takes quite long.
The cat rolls his eyes, as if to declare,
Sometimes we wonder if she needs a spare.

Playing board games, strategy fraught,
With Uncle Joe blundering, he's twisted in knots.
Each roll of the dice ignites new delight,
But when he lands on 'Go to Jail', oh what a sight!

As embers glow softly, we share what was best,
In moments of joy, we are truly blessed.
With giggles like shooting stars, we make our own lore,
In the rhythm of laughter, who could ask for more?

Soft Whispers by the Flame

The fire crackles, sparks take flight,
We tell our tales into the night.
A tale of grandma’s quilted cat,
Who stole our food, imagine that!

A glow of warmth, a cozy cheer,
As funny stories fill the sphere.
Those socks that vanished into thin air,
Where did they go? No one knows where!

We raise our mugs, a toast we make,
To burnt marshmallows and cake mistakes.
With laughter ringing through the room,
And silly hats to chase the gloom.

As shadows dance against the wall,
We leave our cares, both big and small.
Each giggle echoes, bright and clear,
In this warm haven, filled with cheer.

A Gathering of Stars

Beneath the sky, so vast and wide,
We share our dreams, with laughs allied.
A comet darts, like a runaway dog,
Chasing its tail through the heavy fog.

What's that? A shadow by the tree?
Just Uncle Joe, surprised to see!
His fishing pole, all tangled tight,
In fables of fish, he lost the fight.

We count the stars, and guess their names,
Wishing on those silly flames.
One shines bright, as bright as pie,
And someone yells, "Hey, look, a fry!"

So here we bask, in jest and glee,
With tales of things that came to be.
These foolish moments, here to share,
In our galaxy, floating without care.

Toasted Chestnuts and Tales

Around the fire, we gather near,
To share our secrets, sip our beer.
The chestnuts pop, a crackling sound,
As family tales come tumbling down.

Dad once fell into a pile of leaves,
Scaring the cat, who didn't believe.
With every story, laughter grows,
As heartfelt jokes begin to flow.

A cousin's prank, a silly trick,
With whipped cream pies, he sure was quick!
We chase and tumble, laughter spins,
Who needs a board game when this begins?

In cozy moments, we share our fate,
Over toasted chestnuts on a plate.
With each small bite, the memories ignite,
Together we laugh, all through the night.

Echoes of Days Gone By

In days of yore, we danced with glee,
As crazy songs rang out like bees.
Oh, Aunt Barb's wig flew high and wide,
As she twirled round, with flare and pride.

We played charades, our arms like noodles,
Pretending to be one-eyed poodles.
The laughter spilled, like milk on the floor,
As memories blossomed, adding more.

A snapshot caught, our faces a mess,
With chocolate cheeks and silly dress.
Each image tells of a joyful plight,
Reflecting all that felt so right.

So here we sit, in timeless bliss,
With echoes of laughter, who could resist?
In our little nook, stories come alive,
As the past dances, we all revive.

Vaults of Warmth

In this room of giggles, a quirky scene,
A nephew dressed up like a giant green bean.
We can hardly breathe, no one can eat,
As laughter erupts, we shuffle our feet.

The pumpkin pie winks, with whipped cream so high,
Uncle Joe takes a slice, and then starts to fly.
We hold in our snickers while he takes a bite,
And shares a grand tale that goes on all night.

A game of charades, the rules tossed away,
Each gesture so wild, we can’t help but sway.
The clock strikes the hour, but we’re still here,
With remnants of laughter from our hearty cheer.

As the night winds down, hugs all around,
We wrap up our moments, in humor we're bound.
These vaults of warmth, with silliness sprawled,
In the hearts of our clan, we always feel called.

Ties That Endure

In a family gathering, the chaos runs free,
With odd string lights fashioned from a spree.
Mom's quirky decorations block the view,
But we smile and nod, what else can we do?

A cousin who swears he’s the king of the grill,
Flips burgers like magic, yet gives us a thrill.
The fire alarms beep with a spirited shout,
But hey it's still dinner, not a big bout!

We trade all our secrets and games we once played,
Recalling old tales about socks that were frayed.
In laughter we twinkle, as memories weave,
In this tapestry of fun, we all believe.

As the night draws its curtain, the laughter won't fade,
For the ties that we cherish, we've lovingly laid.
With a wink and a hug, we’ll return ever more,
To this joyful chaos, we endlessly adore.

Shadows of the Cozy Past

In the attic, dust bunnies dance,
Old photos laugh at a second chance.
Grandpa's sweater, two sizes too wide,
Critiques the fashion, with pride he'd abide.

Baking cookies that burned like the sun,
Forgotten cinnamon spice—oh what fun!
Cat on the counter, a thief in disguise,
Swiping a treat, oh how he complies!

Sock puppet battles with Grandma's old scarf,
While the dog chews on a comfy old chair half.
The joy in the chaos, the mess and the cheer,
Echoes of laughter fill the atmosphere.

So raise a mug filled with chocolate delight,
To memories shared under soft candlelight.
Each glance back, a giggle, a warm-hearted cheer,
For life's silly moments are treasures so dear.

Songs by the Fireside Glow

By the flames, Uncle Fred sings off-key,
Pets join in, oh, what a cacophony!
The dog howls along, the cat rolls its eyes,
As laughter erupts, the fun multiplies.

Old chairs creak like they're telling a tale,
Of family feuds and a cousin's failed mail.
Hot cocoa spills, a marshmallow mishap,
S’mores stick to our fingers, sticky sweet trap!

A visit from Auntie, she brings her bad puns,
Her “cheesy” jokes, like stale old buns.
We groan and we chuckle, it’s all in good jest,
For moments like these, they truly are blessed.

So let’s hum along 'til the night fades away,
In the cozy glow, where jokes often play.
The music of laughter, our hearts intertwined,
In the warmth of the evening, affection defined.

Tinsel and Time's Gentle Touch

A garland of laughter hangs on the wall,
Remembering times when we'd slip and fall.
A tree with lights that won't stop to twinkle,
Each bulb a reminder of joy's gentle sprinkle.

The cat makes a ladder of ribbons and toys,
While the kids craft a ruckus, oversaturated joys!
Baked pies that collide in a messy blue blur,
Mom's face in disbelief, raising a small slur.

Grandpa shares stories of Christmas gone by,
When socks were stuffed, and we'd all sigh.
With tinsel so bright, our spirits take flight,
In this box of delights, everything feels right.

So toast to the years, to moments we keep,
When laughter and joy fill our hearts, oh so deep.
With each twinkling light, we paint the night bold,
In the tapestry of time, our memories unfold.

Fragments of a Frosty Evening

Snowflakes dance like they’re in a race,
While we build snowmen in a jovial place.
With hats askew and carrot noses askance,
We giggle and tumble, join in the dance.

Frosty air holds whispers of glee,
As hot cocoa warms every nearby knee.
Outdoors we play till our cheeks turn bright,
Retreat to the warmth, our eyes alight.

The fireplace crackles, the marshmallows lend,
To stories retold, family fiends to defend.
A cousin's tall tale? Oh, where will it end?
With laughter erupting—we all just pretend!

So here’s to the evenings we cherish so right,
Each moment a spark, a soft frosty light.
With joy in our hearts, let laughter resound,
In the fragments of fondness, true treasures are found.

Gentle Candles and Memories

The candles flicker, dance, and sway,
My cat thinks they're prey, oh what a play!
She pounces and tumbles, a furry delight,
Chasing shadows in the soft, warm light.

Laughter echoes through the festive air,
With mischief and snacks, we've not a care.
A cake that's lopsided, a pie hit the ground,
Oh, the joy in the chaos, the best moments found!

Uncle Joe's stories never quite land,
He swears his last fish was perfectly planned.
But the punchline is stuck like gum on a shoe,
We laugh till we cry, all true and askew.

Now here's to the moments wrapped up in cheer,
Where glitter and giggles are always near.
We raise our mugs high to the fun that we've spun,
In a whirlwind of memories, we're forever young!

Telling Tales in Twinkle Lights

Twinkle lights hang, they twirl and glide,
Creating a glow where secrets abide.
The stories we share, a mismatched parade,
With ghosts of our past in each memory made.

Aunt Sue spills the beans on that one awkward date,
While Cousin Tim laughs, "You really were late!"
The room fills with giggles as punchlines unfold,
Fueling our warmth like the firelight bold.

Grandpa's old sweater, two sizes too wide,
He insists it's fashion; we all laugh with pride.
Each tale that pops up is a treasure we own,
In our hearts and our laughter, we've truly grown.

So we gather around this festive brigade,
Threading through memories, each one well played.
In twinkle light laughter, our bonds only grow,
With stories and smiles, we embrace the glow!

Evening Embraces

Nighttime wraps us in a cozy embrace,
As caffeine kicks in, oh what a race!
With cookies on plates and jokes running free,
Every smile we share is pure jubilee.

The kids are all buzzing, their energy bright,
Uncle's checking 'round for the last piece of pie and a bite.
Somehow he's tripped, oh what a wild scene,
Rolling and laughing like he's on a screen!

Granny recalls when times were so tough,
Her tales mixed with giggles, she can't get enough.
And we lean in close, soaking up every word,
As the warmth of our laughter is beautifully heard.

So let us gather tight in our evening delight,
With smiles and affection, we'll party all night!
Each hug is a blessing, a joyous release,
In the glow of our laughter, we find our peace.

A Winter's Embrace

Snowflakes are falling, a comedy scene,
Kids bundled up like soft, marshmallow cream.
Dad's on the ground, packing snow for a fight,
With mom as his target, what a funny sight!

The fireplace crackles, a warm, hearty glow,
While grandpa's old quilt makes the ranks overflow.
And out in the yard, what a sight to behold,
A snowman resembling a big lump of gold!

Laughter erupts as traditions collide,
Over cookies and cocoa, we cheekily bide.
Each story shared is a stitch in our heart,
As memories spark joy, that's the best part!

Here's to the winter and all its delight,
With sparkles of laughter that twinkle so bright.
May we savor each moment, in snowflakes and cheer,
With love and pure joy, we'll find winter near!

Threads of Tradition

Grandma's cookies, oh my, what a sight,
The dough sometimes takes off in flight!
With flour on noses, we giggle and cheer,
As we try to bake what she holds dear.

The tree's not straight, oh what a display,
Our ornaments sit in a merry ballet.
There’s a tinsel war, who'll win the crown?
Each strand a battle, we giggle and frown.

Festive sweaters that itch like a goat,
Dad’s dancing moves, we just can't gloat.
With each twirl and skip, he takes a fall,
But laughter reigns, his pride's worth it all.

As snowflakes drift down, we sing out of tune,
Our notes like the laughter, a jubilant boon.
With each precious moment, we find new delight,
In threads of tradition, our hearts soar in flight.

Hearth’s Gentle Serenade

The fire's crackling, popcorn’s a-pop,
We try to roast marshmallows, oh, what a flop!
With sticky fingers and gooey grins wide,
In the dance of the flames, our laughter can't hide.

Uncle Bob’s stories always go on too long,
But if you listen close, there's always a song.
Of mischief and pranks from his youth on the run,
We laugh 'til we cry; he believes he's still young.

The pets are involved, they steal every snack,
With their cute little eyes, they get us off track.
In a tug-of-war, the cat claims our hat,
And we all join in, what a hilarious spat!

These moments together, though silly and sweet,
Remind us that laughter is love's finest treat.
With smiles all around, the evening feels bright,
In the glow of the hearth, our spirits take flight.

Woven Wishes

In our cozy corner, we spin tales anew,
The wackiest wishes, just me and you.
A wish for a cat that can perform tricks,
And maybe a tree that giggles and picks!

We crafted our wishes with laughter and flair,
Imagining snacks that float in the air.
A dance with the fruits, a tango with pies,
In the whirl of our dreams, nothing's a surprise.

The snowman we built, he's a bit out of shape,
With a carrot nose, and a hat made of tape.
He topples, he falls, it's a comical show,
But we roll on the ground, laughing just like it's dough.

With wishes untainted by care or by stress,
Each one a delight, none more or less.
In the warmth of our laughter, our hearts all align,
With woven wishes, we sip on the divine.

Chasing Flickers of Joy

In a flickering glow, we gather around,
With a blanket of giggles, our joy knows no bound.
We'd tell ghost stories but then someone sways,
A shadow that dances, just to set us ablaze!

The lights start to twinkle, and we start to guess,
Which one will flicker? It's a crazy contest!
With bets on a squirrel who scurries in place,
And snacks that disappear, what a funny chase!

The puppy joins in, he thinks it's a race,
With paws in the air, he bounds with such grace.
But trip on a cord, and we all start to shout,
As he tumbles and rolls, joining in on the bout!

With echoes of laughter that shimmer and sway,
We chase all the flickers that brighten our day.
In the warmth of this moment, our hearts feel so light,
As joy weaves its magic, in the soft, starry night.

Luminescence of Laughter

Glowing lights twinkle bright,
Uncle Fred's dance takes flight.
The cat pounces on the tree,
As we all shout, 'Look at me!'

Cookies burn but taste just right,
We laugh through the chef's great fright.
A surprise gift? A rubber chicken,
Now who's laughing? We all kick in!

The tree's crooked, it leans a bit,
Tinsel drapes like a fancy split.
Grandma's socks, they are quite loud,
Her style? She’s always proud!

In this chaos, joy does spark,
Even mischief makes a mark.
With giggles shared, hearts unite,
Merry moments shine so bright!

Nostalgia Wrapped in Red and Gold

The candy canes are all askew,
Dad thought he could paint them blue!
Silly sweaters, oh so bold,
Fashion statements, if truth be told!

Grandpa snored, the lights went dim,
We made a bet, who calls him grim?
Then giggles broke, our secret pact,
A holiday prank—let's reenact!

Mismatched ornaments on display,
Each tells a tale in their own way.
From broken bulbs to glue mishaps,
Our laughter echoes, no time for naps!

Red and gold, a joyful scheme,
In this season, we all dream.
Funny memories gently sway,
Hold them close, come what may!

Pine Scents and Sweet Reminiscence

The scent of pine fills the air,
Mom's secret spice, a fragrant flair.
We argue over who should rake,
But neighbors all hear our loud break!

Mismatched mittens back from the past,
While hot cocoa fills each cup fast.
The snowman leans with a goofy grin,
Oh, the fun; let the chaos begin!

Carols sung off-key tonight,
Even the dog joins in the fright.
Cousins tumble, laughter blooms,
In this haven, joy consumes!

Pine scents swirl through history's gate,
As we dance 'round the fire's fate.
In every giggle, love resides,
Together we find joy abides!

Tales Spun in Twinkling Light

Tales told by the fireplace glow,
Each silly story, stealing the show.
A mishap here with a food fight,
Who knew mashed potatoes could take flight?

Twinkling lights on the window pane,
As we all laugh through the mundane.
One sock missing, that's the game,
We give that gnome all the blame!

Mom dressed in sparkles, what a scene,
Her dance moves? Quite the routine!
With each twirl, we burst with cheer,
In this moment, the world's so near!

Oh, the stories, both old and new,
In laughter's embrace, we know it's true.
With family close and hearts so light,
We weave our tales in twinkling light!

Cherished Moments Under Frost

In the chill of winter's clutch,
We wore socks that drooped and such.
The cat made snowflakes from a star,
While we threw boots and shared a bar.

Laughter echoed in the halls,
As we built our snowman tall.
With carrots stuck and hats askew,
It waved goodbye, our friend so true.

The ice was thick on Grandma's swing,
And Dad fell hard—a comical fling!
The dog barked loud in sheer delight,
As we stumbled home, all frosty and bright.

Through the window, we could spy,
Hot cocoa steaming, oh my, oh my!
Those moments wrapped like scarves around,
In our hearts, their warmth is found.

Recollections in the Ember's Dance

A chair with squeaks, a quilt with stains,
Tales of relatives, their silly gains.
Slippers that squeaked on the wooden floor,
We giggled at stories of 'once more!'

Embers crackled, the shadows played,
As Uncle Joe's grand jokes never swayed.
Bundled in layers, we shared our dreams,
While popcorn bounced—oh, how it screams!

The cat on the mantle, big and proud,
Fell asleep as we roared, oh so loud.
With marshmallow fights, we aimed to land,
In the chaos, there's joy quite unplanned.

Our voices danced with the flames' embrace,
Each memory grinning, found its place.
Though the years will shift like the wind,
The laughter remains—frozen within.

Fireside Murmurs from Long Ago

Grandpa’s stories spun like yarn,
Of ghosts that played and cars that barn.
A chair too small for our dreams to fit,
Yet we giggled beneath the moonlit hit.

Hot dogs roasted on shimmery sticks,
As marshmallows melted, oh, what a mix!
We painted tales with chocolate cheer,
Crafting laughter in the dusk’s black mirror.

Funny faces of shadows cast,
Our giggles echoed, timeless and vast.
Even the dog, with a sly little grin,
Dreamt of s’mores and the fun to win.

Each ember sparked a joke or two,
As the night rolled on in shades of blue.
In a swirl of warmth and slippery treats,
We found the magic in our heartbeat's beats.

The Scent of Spiced Air

From the kitchen, a waft so grand,
Pumpkin pies, oh the perfect plan!
With flour thrown and sugar spilled,
In joyful chaos, our laughter filled.

Fingers sticky with cinnamon dust,
As we whipped up trouble, oh, it was a must!
The recipe lost, but we'll never sway,
For who needs rules on a festive day?

The tree tilted, a sight to behold,
With ornaments dangling—how quite bold!
We laughed at the mischief that dared to strike,
Each memory wrapped in lights we'd hike.

As we sipped cider, warm and bright,
Telling stories that danced through the night,
The spiced air held whispers so sweet,
In the warmth of our hearts, memories greet.

Reflections in the Windowpane

Chubby cheeks and silly hats,
Gingerbread men chasing cats.
Laughter spills like cocoa rich,
As Uncle Fred does a weird twitch.

Frosty noses, snowball fights,
Socks that vanish, oh what delights!
Cousins giggle, hiding behind,
Grandma's tales always unwind.

The lights outside blink in sync,
Dad's latest dance makes us all blink.
With mismatched ornaments proudly hung,
Our off-key carols are sweetly sung.

In the glow of a candle's flick,
A belt snaps loud—it's quite a trick!
Memories stick, like sweet candy canes,
What a riot, this family's reigns!

Joys of the Longest Night

The longest night can't be so bleak,
With dad's old jokes and Auntie's squeak.
We bundle up, all snug and tight,
While siblings feud over the best bite.

Grandpa's snores shake the floors,
We sneak on tipsy, opening drawers.
Candies stolen, pillows tossed,
In this fluffy chaos, we're all lost.

The fire crackles, stories told,
What's that? A shadow? Oh, so bold!
A ghost? A bear? Or just a cat?
We scream and giggle—imagine that!

As midnight strikes with silent cheer,
The kitchen's filled with festive beer.
With belly laughs and merry jest,
This night, my friends, is simply the best!

Whispers of Winter's Glow

Snowflakes dance as we build,
A snowman shaped like Uncle Will.
He has a carrot, sad and short,
As we pretend he’ll play croquet court.

The fireplace crackles as flames leap,
While secrets are shared, a giggle sheep.
Mom’s pie cooling on the side,
It’s a wonder she hasn’t cried!

The lights twinkle, the world’s aglow,
We pretend we’re in a winter show.
With hot chocolate, whipped cream’s a must,
Grandma says it’s our little trust.

We toast with marshmallows, reach for the sky,
And dare each other to whisper 'why.'
For in this mirth, we feel so bold,
These whispers of joy turn to gold!

Embered Echoes

The fireplace pops as logs embrace,
A puppy darts all over the place.
Laughter echoes in every nook,
Dad just can’t give that cookie a look.

Christmas sweaters, bright and grand,
With reindeer prancing across the land.
Auntie’s hat, so bright it glows,
She tripped on the cat’s little toes.

What’s the game we’ll play tonight?
While grandpa snores, we take flight.
We sneak and peek around the bend,
Among these echoes, we’re all friends.

As coals warm slowly, and giggles rise,
Through windowpanes, we see the skies.
So bring on joy, let the laughter swell,
In embered echoes, all is well!

Comfort in the Chill

When winter comes and snowflakes fall,
I search for snacks, not gifts at all.
The fridge is bare, the cupboard sighs,
A popcorn ball is my best prize.

We huddle close by fireside glow,
With fuzzy socks and tales aglow.
But Auntie Edna’s fruitcake fright,
Might haunt my dreams all through the night.

Hot cocoa steams in mugs too small,
As we recount the time I tripped and sprawled.
The laughter echoes, warm and clear,
'Til all my woes just disappear.

So here’s to warmth, the giggles shared,
And all the moments showing we cared.
When winter chills and snowflakes twirl,
We find our joy, let laughter whirl.

The Heart of the Home

Amidst the clutter, toys abound,
The heart of home can still be found.
With cookies baking, sugar high,
And little hands that swipe and try.

The table spreads with sticky treats,
Where every bite is more than sweets.
Uncle's jokes bring quite the groan,
As we hold tight to silly tone.

Grandma’s quilt, a cozy mess,
A fort made out of pure finesse.
The dog bumps in, his tail a blur,
While chaos waves, we all concur.

So gather close, embrace the fun,
In laughter’s warmth, we’re never done.
Home is not just roof and wall,
It’s loving hearts and joyful call.

Pinecone Pathways

On pinecone trails, we roam and race,
With sticky pine sap on our face.
The squirrels watch, bemused and sly,
As we try to leap, but only fly.

In winter's clutch, we gather round,
With twigs and tales that know no bound.
The crafting moments pure delight,
As glitter flies in soft twilight.

With marshmallow fights and laughter sweet,
And cookies left for Santa's feet.
Each stumble met with gleeful cheer,
As memories bloom through smiles so clear.

So here's the cheer, let spirits soar,
In every mishap, we crave for more.
With pinecone trails, our hearts will race,
In playful joy, we find our place.

Whispers Against the Wind

The wind it howls with secrets bold,
As socks disappear from stories told.
While laughter rings and stories spin,
Of all the times we took a win.

The chilly air brings noses red,
With hot soup served from a giant spread.
And crafty kids with glittered hands,
Paint dreams while plotting snowy lands.

As shadows dance, old tales arise,
Of the great cat who stole our fries.
With every giggle that breaks the calm,
The spirit stirs, like a cozy balm.

So let the whispers guide us near,
To gather treasures bright and dear.
In frost-kissed nights, with hearts a-blend,
We find our joy that never ends.

Milton Keynes UK
Ingram Content Group UK Ltd.
UKHW021242191124
451300UK00007B/192

9 789916 941102